34880000822937

BOOK CHARGING CARD

974.2

Accession No. _____ Call No. CRA

Author *Craats, Rennay*

Title *New Hampshire*

974.2 CRA

Craats, Rennay

New Hampshire

34880000 822937

NEW HAMPSHIRE

Rennay Craats

Published by Weigl Publishers Inc.
123 South Broad Street, Box 227
Mankato, MN 56002
USA
Web site: http://www.weigl.com

Library of Congress Cataloging-in-Publication Data available upon request from the publisher. Fax: (507) 388-2746 for the attention of the Publishing Records Department.

ISBN 1-59036-001-X

Printed in the United States of America
1 2 3 4 5 6 7 8 9 10   05 04 03 02 01

Project Coordinator
Michael Lowry
Substantive Editor
Michelle Lomberg
Copy Editor
Heather Kissock
Designers
Warren Clark
Terry Paulhus
Layout
Katherine Phillips
Photo Researcher
Gayle Murdoff

Photograph Credits
Every reasonable effort has been made to trace ownership and to obtain permission to reprint copyright material. The publishers would be pleased to have any errors or omissions brought to their attention so that they may be corrected in subsequent printings.

Cover: Granite (Steve Mulligan Photography), Tugboats (Ralph Morang Photography); **America's Stonehenge:** page 12T; **Corel Corporation:** pages 5T, 5B, 9B, 10T, 11B, 13B, 23T, 28T, 28B, 29L; **Bettman/Corbis:** page 17T; **EyeWire Corporation:** page 14B; **Ralph Morang Photography:** pages 3T, 4B, 6T, 7B, 8T, 10B, 11T, 12B, 14T, 20T, 20B, 21B, 22, 24T; **Steve Mulligan Photography:** pages 4T, 7T; **National Archives of Canada C-13320:** page 17B; **New Hampshire Historical Society:** pages 16T, 16B, 18T, 18B, 19T, 19B; **Courtesy of Northeastern Imaging:** page 23B (Sean Reid); **Photodisc Corporation:** page 15B; **Photofest:** page 25B; **Courtesy of State of New Hampshire Office of Travel and Tourist Development:** pages 3M, 3B, 8B, 9T, 13T, 21T, 24B, 26T, 26B, 27T, 27B, 29R; **David Sturges:** page 15T.

CONTENTS

New Hampshire was once home to more than 400 covered bridges. Nearly 350 of the bridges have been destroyed by flooding or fires.

INTRODUCTION

New Hampshire is one of the original thirteen colonies and the birthplace of some of the most important democratic events in the history of the United States. On January 5, 1776, New Hampshire adopted its own **constitution** and became the first state to declare independence from Great Britain. New Hampshire's announcement came 6 months before the official Declaration of Independence.

Since 1920, the long road to the White House has begun in New Hampshire. Every 4 years, this quiet New England state becomes the focus of the nation's attention. During presidential elections, New Hampshire is the first state in the nation to hold its **presidential primary election**. New Hampshirites take their role seriously and have one of the highest voter turnouts in the country.

QUICK FACTS

Captain John Mason named the state after the British town of Hampshire. He lived in Hampshire as a young man.

The official state song is "Old New Hampshire," but there are another eight **honorary** state songs as well.

Concord is New Hampshire's capital city.

New Hampshire is one of six New England states. The other states are Connecticut, Maine, Massachusetts, Rhode Island, and Vermont.

In 1860, Abraham Lincoln launched his presidential campaign in New Hampshire.

New Hampshire's 13-mile coastline is the shortest coastline in the country.

New Hampshire has more than 220 miles of federal interstate highways.

Getting There

New Hampshire is located in the northeastern United States. To the east lie Maine and the waters of the Atlantic Ocean. Massachusetts forms New Hampshire's southern border, and Vermont makes up its western edge. The state shares its northern border with the Canadian province of Quebec.

Getting to New Hampshire is as easy as boarding a plane or climbing into a car. More than 15,000 miles of highway carry traffic into and out of the state. For air travelers, Manchester Airport, the state's largest airport, is a major destination. In addition, there are more than ninety other airports in the state. While New Hampshire's miles of railroad tracks are used less today than in the past, some trains still offer sightseeing trips. These trips provide visitors with a memorable way to experience New Hampshire.

QUICK FACTS

New Hampshire joined the Union on June 21, 1788. It was the ninth state to become part of the United States of America.

In 1955, the last passenger train in New Hampshire stopped running in Warner. The last freight train quit 6 years later.

The state flag has the state seal in the center of a blue background. Nine stars represent the nine states of the Union when New Hampshire joined.

New Hampshire Location Map

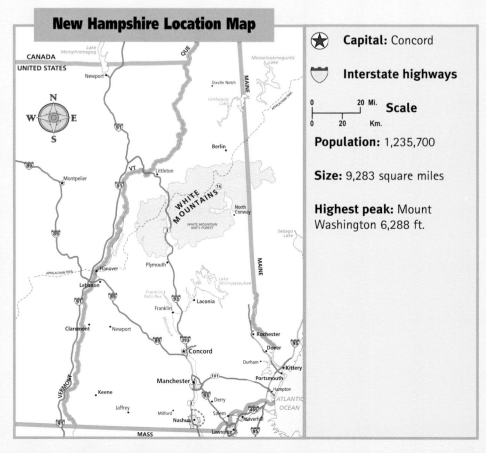

Capital: Concord

Interstate highways

Scale
0   20 Mi.
0   20 Km.

Population: 1,235,700

Size: 9,283 square miles

Highest peak: Mount Washington 6,288 ft.

New Hampshire played a major role in the American Revolution. As early as December 1774, rebels began fighting against British rule. The rebels forced the British-appointed governor, John Wentworth, out of the colony, and a new **revolutionary** government took over. While no battles took place in the state during the American Revolution, it was important to the cause. Portsmouth became a key town in the war. From there, about 100 privately owned vessels were launched in attacks against British ships. New Hampshirites also came to the aid of Massachusetts rebels during the battles of Lexington and Concord in 1775.

During the American Revolution, New Hampshire contributed three army regiments to the Continental Army.

New Hampshire supplied several strong military leaders to the **Continental Army**, including John Stark and John Sullivan. John Stark's regiment helped defend Bunker Hill, and Stark led troops, together with John Sullivan, in the battles of Trenton in 1776 and Princeton in 1777. In August 1777, Stark and his men helped turn the tide of the war when they prevented the British forces from stealing much-needed supplies at Bennington. Then, in 1779, Sullivan defeated a powerful British force and its Iroquois supporters at Newtown, New York.

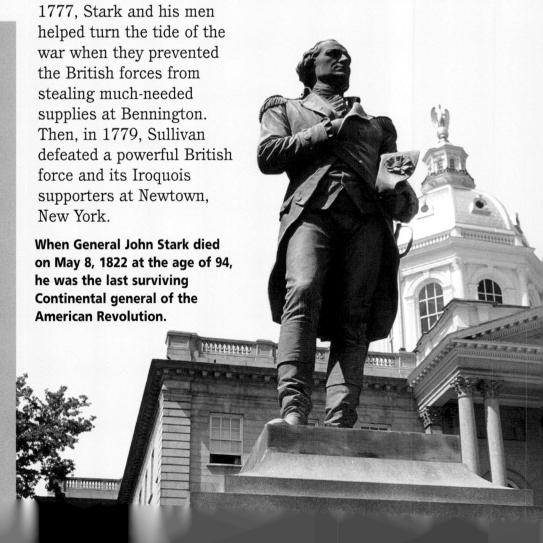

When General John Stark died on May 8, 1822 at the age of 94, he was the last surviving Continental general of the American Revolution.

QUICK FACTS

It was New Hampshire's vote on June 21, 1788 that put the United States Constitution into effect.

General Stark toasted his soldiers during a reunion of the Battle of Bennington, encouraging them to "Live Free or Die." This became the state motto.

New Hampshire's earth symbols celebrate the state's unique geology. The official gem is smoky quartz, the official mineral is **beryl**, and the official rock is granite.

New Hampshire's lakes are some of the most beautiful in New England. The warm waters of Lake Winnipesaukee, Lake Sunapee, and Newfound Lake draw swimmers and sunbathers from miles around.

New Hampshire has approximately forty rivers, which cover about 41,800 miles.

Until about 10,000 years ago, all of New Hampshire was buried beneath **glaciers**. These glaciers created the amazing landscape found in the state. The glaciers chiseled and molded the mountains. As these ice masses melted, they created countless lakes, streams, and rivers. The "Mother of Rivers" state nickname recognizes that five of the large New England streams start in the granite hills of New Hampshire. It is also a reflection of the hundreds of lakes, ponds, and rivers found throughout the state.

New Hampshire's other nicknames also refer to the distinct landscapes found in the state. Plentiful granite deposits established New Hampshire as "The Granite State." "The White Mountain State" draws attention to the grand and rugged mountain range in the northern part of the state. Lastly, New Hampshire is often referred to as the "Switzerland of America" because of the stunning mountain scenery matched only by the Alps.

QUICK FACTS

Water is important in New Hampshire. The state has more than 1,300 lakes and ponds.

Space fascinates many New Hampshirites. Alan Shepard, the first person from the United States to travel in space, was from East Derry. Christa McAuliffe, a New Hampshire social studies teacher, died when the space shuttle *Challenger* exploded in 1986.

The highest point in the state is Mount Washington. It is 6,288 feet tall.

New Hampshire is approximately 180 miles long and 50 miles wide.

Small white churches are a common sight along New Hampshire's countryside roads.

The "Old Man of the Mountain" is a rocky outcropping on Profile Mountain that resembles the face of a man.

LAND AND CLIMATE

New Hampshire consists of three main geographic regions—the White Mountains, the New England Upland, and the Seaboard Lowland. The White Mountains cross the northern part of the state. Forested valleys and rugged uplands provide ample opportunities for hiking and bird-watching. Most of the southern and central part of the state is in the New England Upland region. The rolling hills of this region are dotted with lakes and crisscrossed by rivers. Lastly, the Seaboard Lowland, in southeastern New Hampshire, slopes gently toward the Atlantic coastline.

In July, temperatures range from 63° Fahrenheit in the north to 70°F in the south. In January, the average temperature is between 12°F in the north and 26°F on the coast. New Hampshirites are expert shovelers, as heavy snowfalls are common during winter.

New Hampshire has some of the coldest winters in the eastern United States.

The Basin at Franconia Notch State Park is more than 20 feet wide. It was carved out of the rock by a waterfall.

NATURAL RESOURCES

With a nickname like "The Granite State," it makes sense that granite is a top natural resource in New Hampshire. Granite—which is a very hard, gray stone—is one of the most important and valuable minerals in New Hampshire. Nearly every county has a granite **quarry**. A great deal of the granite mined in New Hampshire is used in construction. Other valuable minerals in the state are sand and gravel. These are found throughout New Hampshire and make up more than half of the state's mineral output.

Another natural resource that gives the state economy a boost is forestry. Timber is used largely in the pulp and paper industry. It is also used to build such products as **railroad ties**, fence posts, and furniture.

QUICK FACTS

Large deposits of sand and gravel were left behind by melting glaciers.

Clay and gemstones are also important to the state economy.

During the colonial period, stagecoaches and the masts on warships were built using New Hampshire timber.

Forestry contributes about $3.9 billion to New Hampshire's economy each year.

To help preserve New Hampshire's forests, the state government taxes timber only after it has been cut.

The forestry industry in New Hampshire employs about 16,000 people.

PLANTS AND ANIMALS

Asters bloom in late summer, which provides bees and other insects with nectar and pollen as they prepare for winter.

New Hampshire is the second most forested state in the country, after Maine. More than 82 percent of New Hampshire's land is covered in trees. Evergreen forests of spruce and fir trees blanket the north, and white pine, maple, and oak trees cover parts of southern and central New Hampshire. The state's official tree is the white birch.

Hundreds of different wildflowers cover the forest floors, including wild asters, black-eyed Susans, daisies, and buttercups. The pink lady slipper is the official wildflower of the state. This flower is native to New Hampshire and grows well in the moist, wooded areas of the state. The state's official flower, the purple lilac, is relatively new to New Hampshire. It was brought from Britain and planted at Governor Wentworth's home in 1750. It was chosen as the state flower because it is hardy and strong, just like New Hampshirites.

QUICK FACTS

Many different shrubs take root beneath the state's trees. The American yew, red osier, mountain laurel, and hobblebush shrubs are all common throughout New Hampshire.

There are forty-three state parks, thirty-nine islands, fourteen natural areas, and seven recreation trails in New Hampshire.

White birch trees, which can grow to be 80 feet tall, are also known as canoe or paper birches. The bark of the tree peels in thin layers and was once used as writing paper and for making canoes.

The purple lilac became New Hampshire's state flower on January 9, 1919.

Loons are excellent divers. They can hold their breath underwater for more than 1 minute.

A variety of animals roam New Hampshire's wilderness areas. Of the large animals in the state, the white-tailed deer is the most common. Snowshoe hares, mice, shrews, and squirrels all call the state home. Other animals common to New Hampshire include beavers, bears, moose, porcupines, minks, foxes, and bobcats. New Hampshire is also home to some unusual animals. The spotted newt, for example, is the official state amphibian. The skin of young spotted newts is toxic, and their bright red color serves as a warning to stay away.

New Hampshirites have plenty of bird-watching opportunities. Black-capped chickadees, woodpeckers, and white-throated sparrows can all be found in the state. Other birds, including the loon, the northern harrier, and the woodcock, have declining populations that concern conservationists at the refuge.

New Hampshire's waterways are brimming with fish. Lake trout and landlocked salmon swim the state's deep lakes, while bass, pickerel, and perch make their homes in the state's shallow lakes and ponds.

Bobcats are named for their short tail, which resembles a bob or a knob. Bobcats commonly weigh up to 30 pounds.

America's Stonehenge, in New Salem, is more than 4,000 years old and is the nation's oldest stone construction.

TOURISM

Every summer, more than 1 million people visit New Hampshire to enjoy its picturesque beauty and outdoor activities. One tourist destination is filled with mystery. Known as America's Stonehenge, this ancient structure combines astronomy with stone masonry. While no one knows for certain how the stone maze got there or which civilization built it, many archeologists believe that it may have been a prehistoric calendar used by Native Americans. The structure can still be used to determine solar and lunar events during the year. Historic artifacts found at America's Stonehenge, such as pottery, tools, and scripts, have fascinated archeologists and visitors to New Hampshire for decades.

Another huge hit with tourists is Six Gun City and Fort Splash Water Park in Jefferson. There, visitors get a taste of the Old West—they are invited to pan for gemstones, help the sheriff catch outlaws, and inspect vehicles from the 1800s. The amusement park has a large selection of water rides, including water coasters, bumper boats, pedal boats, and waterslides.

QUICK FACTS

The Greenville Wildlife Park is a must-see for young and old alike. This park, the only one of its kind in the state, enables people to see such exotic animals as tigers and lions in their natural environments. It also teaches visitors about endangered species.

The Town of Newbury established a creative tourism center in 1999. It is housed in the **caboose** of an old train.

The American Independence Museum in Exeter follows the transformation of one town from the American Revolution into the twentieth century.

The American Independence Museum provides an interactive look at colonial life during the American Revolution.

Between the months of March and April, New Hampshire produces almost 90,000 gallons of maple syrup.

QUICK FACTS

The Belknap Mill, in Laconia, once supported a bustling mill industry. Built in 1823, it is the oldest unchanged brick textile mill in the United States.

Nursery and greenhouse products, Christmas trees, and apples are the main crops grown in the state. Hay, which is primarily used to feed livestock, is a valuable field crop. Many nurseries raise seedlings and flowers for cities such as New York and Boston.

It is not easy to tap maple trees. It takes about 40 gallons of sap to make about 1 gallon of maple syrup. Cold nights and warm days are needed for the sap to "run."

INDUSTRY

Trees are the source of a valuable industry in New Hampshire. For 6 weeks every year, between 600 and 1,000 farmers tap maple trees for sap to make maple sugar, sugar candies, and maple syrup. This growing industry contributes more than $4 million per year to the state's economy.

Agriculture is another important industry in the state. There are more than 2,500 farms spread across New Hampshire, totaling 420,000 acres of land. The dairy industry generates about $44 million each year. Fresh milk from the region is drunk locally or shipped to markets in Massachusetts. Farmers across the country and beyond envy New Hampshire's top-notch dairy cows. These cows are sold as breeding animals around the world. Dairy cattle are the main livestock raised in New Hampshire, but farmers also raise beef cattle, chickens, turkeys, and hogs.

New Hampshire's 20,000 dairy cows produce more than 41 million gallons of milk per year.

Each year, New Hampshire produces more than $7 billion worth of manufactured goods.

GOODS AND SERVICES

Manufactured goods are a crucial part of New Hampshire's economy. Industrial machinery is the top manufactured product. The state produces a variety of different types of industrial machinery, including computers and computer products, machinery for the pulp and paper industry, and bearings. Other important manufactured goods are paper products, rubber and plastic products, magazines and newspapers, and metals.

High-technology is a booming industry in New Hampshire. Companies such as Photran are devoted to producing circuit boards, optical fiber cables, and semiconductors. The state has the highest percentage of high-technology workers in the country. Many New Hampshirites are trained to make precision tools, including electricity-measuring devices, surgical tools, and optical lenses and instruments.

New Hampshire is an important center for the manufacturing of circuit boards. Circuit boards are the building blocks of many everyday objects, including calculators and cellular telephones.

QUICK FACTS

In the 1950s, the USS *Albacore* was the fastest submarine ever designed. It was built at the Portsmouth Naval Shipyard.

The Seabrook nuclear power plant provides more than half of the state's electricity. About 40 percent of the electricity generated in New Hampshire comes from coal- and oil-burning plants. The rest is generated by **hydroelectric** plants.

Flounder, smelt, lobster, shrimps, and crabs are all valuable fishing products in New Hampshire's small fishing industry.

There are more than 1,000 software companies in New Hampshire.

The State Library, in Concord, is the largest public library in New Hampshire.

While many residents work in the manufacturing sector, a large portion of the population works to perform services for others. Many of the state's service employees work in tourism. These people include servers and chefs in restaurants, ticket-takers at amusement parks, and hotel staff. Not all service workers cater to tourists. Government officials, teachers, doctors, accountants, and lawyers all work in the service industry.

Many New Hampshirites like to stay well informed. It is easy to do given the high-quality newspapers, radio stations, and television stations available throughout the state. The *New Hampshire Gazette* was the first newspaper in the state. It later evolved into the *Portsmouth Herald*. There are eight daily newspapers, including Manchester's *Union Leader*, Nashua's *Telegraph*, and Concord's *Monitor*. In addition to print media, there are twenty-seven AM and thirty-five FM radio stations, as well as six television stations.

More than 240,000 people in New Hampshire work in the service industry.

FIRST NATIONS

Before European explorers arrived, there were approximately 12,000 Native Peoples living in the New Hampshire area. Most of these people were Algonquian speakers, including people of the Abenaki and Pennacook groups. The number of Native Peoples in the region dropped dramatically in the 1600s due in part to fierce battles with the Mohawk to the west. Both the Abenaki and Pennacook lived by hunting, fishing, and farming. Many Native-American hunting grounds spread into what are today western Maine and the lower Connecticut Valley.

The Native Peoples made their homes, called **wigwams**, out of tree bark and animal skins. The Pennacook often built their villages around farms. In summer, they moved to the coastal areas to fish. As the number of animals or fish in an area decreased, the Native groups moved on to more plentiful areas.

Before the arrival of European settlers, many Native Americans hunted fish with bows and arrows.

The Abenaki belong to a collection of Native-American groups known as the Wabanaki, whose name means "People of the First Light" or "Dawnland."

In addition to being an adventurous explorer, Captain John Smith was also a well-known mapmaker and an author of exciting travelers' tales.

EXPLORERS AND MISSIONARIES

The first Europeans to land in New Hampshire were most likely Viking sailors in the eleventh century. There may also have been English fishers exploring the North American oceans as early as the fifteenth century. However, the first recorded exploration of the region was made by Englishman Martin Pring in 1603. He sailed up the Piscataqua River and is thought to have come ashore at what is now Portsmouth.

Pring was not alone in his interest of the area. In 1605, French explorer Samuel de Champlain arrived in the area and mapped the region's coastline. Then in 1614, English captain John Smith landed on the Isles of Shoals. He mapped the area for England.

Britain had great interest in the area. In 1619, King James I established a Council for New England. He wanted to encourage people to settle in the region. Soon, small groups of settlers were sailing across the ocean to make a new life in New Hampshire.

Today, Samuel de Champlain's map of the eastern seaboard is considered a work of genius and a national treasure.

QUICK FACTS

Captain Pring did not venture far into New Hampshire. He explored the coastline and a short distance into the interior of the region.

After establishing a settlement in Jamestown, Virginia, in 1607, Captain John Smith spent many years surveying unexplored parts of New England. His book, *A Description of New England*, led the pilgrims to Massachusetts.

The Isles of Shoals were once named Smith's Islands, after explorer John Smith.

EARLY SETTLERS

The English government issued many overlapping and confusing land grants in the New Hampshire region. In 1622, Captain John Mason and Sir Ferdinando Gorges were both given grants for the land between the Kennebec and Merrimack Rivers. The two men split the land between them at the Piscataqua River. Gorges called his eastern region Piscataqua, which became the province of Maine. Mason named his region New Hampshire.

Scotsman David Thompson and a group of settlers were given permission to colonize a smaller piece of land in the New Hampshire area. In 1623, they arrived near present-day Portsmouth and created a settlement called Odiorne's Point. There, they cleared farmland and began fishing the waters. Odiorne's Point is now part of Rye.

Captain John Mason spent thousands of dollars to help the settlers of New Hampshire clear land and build houses.

Captain John Mason established New Hampshire as a fishing colony in 1623.

Robert Rogers was the leader of Rogers' Rangers, a group of British soldiers who were scouts during the French and Indian Wars.

In 1638, the towns of Exeter and Hampton were established. Dover, Portsmouth, Hampton, and Exeter were the only permanent settlements in the area until 1673. Simple settlements soon developed into towns, which began to spread along the river banks. During the mid- to late-1600s, New Hampshire was often governed by Massachusetts, and the two colonies shared the same royal governor until 1741. In 1741, New Hampshire became independent of Massachusetts and was given its own royal governor.

During the French and Indian Wars, many New Hampshirites joined the fight and became important military leaders. By the 1760s, British rule had worn thin with the colonists. New Hampshirites took up arms against Britain and battled eight years for independence. Once independent, New Hampshire's trade and economy soared, and more people rushed to the state to find work and start a new life.

QUICK FACTS

Robert Rogers and John Stark were brave New Hampshirites who helped defeat French forces during the French and Indian Wars.

In 1732, the population of New Hampshire was about 12,500 people. By 1790, the number of people living in the region had jumped to 141,885.

New Hampshire was the only one of the original thirteen colonies that the British did not invade during the American Revolution.

John Stark was highly respected among revolutionary officers for his ability to predict the enemy's military movements.

The city of Dover, established in 1623, is known as New Hampshire's oldest permanent settlement.

POPULATION

In the mid-1800s, many of the people in New Hampshire were of British **ancestry**. As the state became more and more industrialized, new people moved there to work in the booming factories and mills. Since that time, the population has continued to grow. For example, between 1980 and 1990, New Hampshire's population swelled by more than 20 percent, boasting one of the most dramatic increases in the United States. By the end of 2000, there were more than 1.2 million Americans living within New Hampshire's borders.

New Hampshirites tend to be young and well educated. About 25 percent of the population is below the age of 18. Nearly 15 percent of people 25 years of age and older in the state are college graduates.

Nearly 60 percent of people in New Hampshire live in cities.

QUICK FACTS

The smallest town in the state is New Castle. It covers only 0.8 square miles and has a population of 800 people.

Most people in New Hampshire were born in the United States. About 96 percent of the population is of European descent, 1.3 percent is Asian American, and 0.7 percent is African American.

The population density of New Hampshire is about 138 people per square mile of land. The average for the nation is 77 people per square mile.

The most populated cities in New Hampshire are Manchester, Nashua, Concord, and Portsmouth.

The State House was finished in 1819. This elegant building is made of marble and granite.

POLITICS AND GOVERNMENT

New Hampshire's government is made up of three main branches—the executive, legislative, and judicial. The governor and the Executive Council are part of the executive branch. The governor cannot spend money without the council's approval. The executive branch ensures that laws are carried out.

The legislative branch is made up of 24 senators and 400 members of the House of Representatives. The state's House of Representatives has more members than any other state in the country. It brings new laws into play and changes or updates old ones. Both the Senate and the House of Representatives need to agree on a bill before it is forwarded to the governor for approval.

The third branch, the judicial, is made up of the courts. The highest court is the Supreme Court, which consists of a chief justice and four associate judges. There are lower district and municipal courts in this branch as well. The judicial branch is in charge of enforcing and interpreting state laws.

QUICK FACTS

New Hampshire's constitution was enacted in 1784, making it the second oldest in the United States.

Besides New Hampshire, Massachusetts is the only other state with an Executive Council. This five-member body can overrule the governor in most cases.

Franklin Pierce was a war hero and the youngest elected president of the United States in his time. Born in Hillsboro, Pierce served as president from 1853 to 1857.

New Hampshire has 10 counties, 13 municipalities, and 221 towns.

New Hampshire's legislative branch is also known as the General Court.

Franklin Pierce was the first citizen of New Hampshire to be elected president of the United States. He was born in 1804.

CULTURAL GROUPS

As New Hampshire developed into an industrial center in the early twentieth century, it was flooded with people from all over the globe. Immigrants, especially those from Scotland, England, Holland, France, Poland, Greece, Ireland, and Canada, provided the rapidly growing industries with an inexpensive work force. This steady flow of immigrants to New Hampshire, which lasted until the 1920s, also created a **diverse** and exciting culture in the state.

As more immigrants arrived in an area, they began forming ethnic neighborhoods. In this new country, newcomers could find a community that spoke their native language, ate familiar foods, and understood the customs and traditions with which they had grown up. These unique neighborhoods boasted markets carrying specialty cultural goods. Many also used their native language as well as English on store signs. Some ethnic areas, including the German, Hispanic, and French neighborhoods, grew quickly and worked hard to preserve their heritage. They continue to do so today.

The caber toss is a popular event at New Hampshire's Scottish Highland Festival. Many of the logs tossed into the air weigh more than 130 pounds.

QUICK FACTS

Many New Hampshirites are descendents of English and Scottish settlers. Most live on the same property or in the same houses that their ancestors did.

The largest ethnic groups in New Hampshire are Scottish and English. Other prominent groups in the state include French, Hispanic, Native American, Chinese, African American, and Asian.

Some New Hampshire mill owners recruited workers straight from the immigration center on Ellis Island in New York.

Pasta noodles are a traditional Italian food and are available at markets throughout New Hampshire.

Some New Hampshirites celebrate their culture through food. Ethnic restaurants offer delicious dishes from countries such as China, Italy, Poland, and Greece. Other groups celebrate their culture through music and dancing. Morris dancing is an old English form of dancing that is practiced in southwestern New Hampshire. This lively dance is performed for an audience and is thought to be a celebration of spring. The dancers, accompanied by a live musician, wear bells on their legs and wave sticks and handkerchiefs. Teams of morris dancers often tour New England, with each team having their own special "kit," or uniform.

People need not be from another country to enjoy traditional dancing. Contra dancing is enjoyed in every county in New Hampshire. For more than 200 years, people in New Hampshire have participated in contra dancing. This exciting dance is led by a caller and is danced in a long line with a partner. By the end of the dance, each person has danced with all other dancers in the line.

Contra dancing was originally made popular by Queen Elizabeth I, who introduced the dance to her court in the sixteenth century.

Ballet New England regularly performs classic ballets, such as *Swan Lake* and *The Nutcracker*.

QUICK FACTS

Sarah Josepha Hale was an author and journalist from Newport. Her well-known poem *Mary Had a Little Lamb* was first published in 1830.

Arts Jubilee is an annual summer concert series held in North Conway Village. Every Thursday evening in July and August, the Arts Jubilee presents musical acts ranging from Celtic to classical. Other musical events include the Lake Winnipesaukee Music Festival and the New Hampshire Music Festival.

J.D. Salinger, author of the legendary yet controversial novel *Catcher in the Rye*, lived in New Hampshire.

Two of John Irving's novels, *The World According to Garp* and *The Cider House Rules*, have been made into successful movies.

ARTS AND ENTERTAINMENT

New Hampshire has been home to many successful writers. Among them is novelist John Irving. Born in Exeter, Irving wrote his first novel in 1969. By 1978, he had reached the top with his popular fourth novel, *The World According to Garp*. *The Hotel New Hampshire*, *The Cider House Rules*, *A Prayer for Owen Meany*, and *A Widow for One Year* have all brought great success to the talented author. They have also brought recognition to his home state, in which many of his novels are set.

Music and dance are also popular arts in the state. Ballet New England, in Portsmouth, stages ballet performances throughout the year. Several orchestras, including the Monadnock Chorus and Orchestra and the New Hampshire Philharmonic Orchestra in Manchester, keep classical music lovers' toes tapping. The superior acoustics of Music Hall in Portsmouth guarantees an unbeatable performance by the many talented musicians, actors, and dancers who grace its stage. Music Hall brings exciting touring productions to New Hampshire.

The lively performances of the "The Pittsfield Players" make them a popular theatrical attraction for New Hampshire audiences.

In its heyday in the 1950s and 1960s, the Hampton Playhouse was the place to be from July through September. This seaside summer theater attracted some of Hollywood's and Broadway's biggest stars. The theater closed down in 2001.

The Cornish Hill Pottery Company is well-known for its stoneware. The handcrafted pots are decorated with the same technique used by early North American and European potters—a method called "slip trailing." A creamy clay and water mixture, called the slip, is put on nearly hardened pots, which adds a natural color to the pieces.

In Holderness, film buffs can take a sailing tour to view the sights featured in the Oscar-winning film *On Golden Pond*.

New Hampshirites crowd theaters throughout the state to experience excellent live drama. The Seacoast Repertory Theater is one of the top regional theaters in the area. There, the Portsmouth Academy of Performing Arts and the Portsmouth Youth Theater work year-round to present musicals and dramas. They are often the first to present works by new playwrights. The Celebrity Series in Durham also presents world-class dance, music, and theater.

The numerous art galleries and museums in New Hampshire feature local and international works of art. Some of the best in the state include the Hood Museum of Art in Dartmouth and the Currier Gallery of Art in Manchester.

Over the years, New Hampshire has seen its share of Hollywood celebrities. Such legends as Henry Fonda and Katherine Hepburn have experienced the majestic beauty of New Hampshire. Squam Lake was the setting for many scenes in the duo's 1981 classic movie *On Golden Pond*.

Katherine Hepburn and Henry Fonda won best actress and best actor Oscars for their roles in *On Golden Pond*.

New Hampshire's official state sport is skiing.

SPORTS

New Hampshirites are kept busy with the state's many facilities and recreation areas. Cycling is a popular way to see the area and get some exercise. Mountain bikers can explore the trails through the White Mountains and through parks such as the Franconia Notch State Park. For those who prefer to have their feet on the ground, hiking is an exciting sport in New Hampshire. Trails wind up to the top of the White Mountain peaks, offering hikers sensational views and a glimpse of the area's wildlife.

More than 2 million skiers and snowboarders travel to New Hampshire each year to test their skills on the slopes. Attitash Bear Peak is the largest ski resort in the state. Skiers also visit Black Mountain, Cannon Mountain, Cranmore, and Shawnee Peak for a challenge. For those who prefer flatter terrain, Jackson offers some of the best cross-country skiing in the eastern United States.

Mountain biking is a great way to tour New Hampshire's White Mountain Range.

An extensive network of hiking paths connects virtually every peak of New Hampshire's White Mountain Range.

New Hampshire athletes do not compete in professional leagues, but that does not mean there is a shortage of sports. The University of New Hampshire Wildcats fill arenas with cheering fans when they take to the football and soccer fields, skate onto the ice in hockey, or suit up for basketball and volleyball. Many Wildcats players have been awarded national prizes and have enjoyed professional careers in their sports. The football team was proud to see players such as Ryan Ward drafted by the Chicago Bears and Dan Kreider wearing a Pittsburgh Steelers uniform.

On the soccer pitch, the university boasts heroes, with Adam Purcell named the 1999 American East Player of the Year. Before him, Mike Veneto took the award in 1993 and 1994. In 1999, Purcell dominated the game and led the league in goals with twenty-one. The Wildcats' hockey goalie Ty Conklin has twice been nominated for the Hobey Baker Award, which is presented to the top college hockey player in the country. Throughout his schooling at the university, he broke goaltending records and was named the 2000 Hockey East Player of the Year.

Kayaking is a popular adventure sport enjoyed by many people looking for a unique way to explore New Hampshire's outdoors.

Brain Teasers

1

What did New Hampshire have to do with the Russo-Japanese War?

Answer: The treaty that ended the war was negotiated in Portsmouth. New Hampshire is the only state to ever be part of the conclusion of a foreign war.

2

Where was the first potato planted in the United States?

Answer: The first potato planted in the country was at Londonderry Common Field in 1719.

3

How did skiing come to New Hampshire?

Answer: In the late 1800s, when Scandinavian settlers arrived in the state, they brought their skis with them. By the 1920s, skiing was an important sport in New Hampshire.

4

What is the Great Bay Estuary?

Answer: The Great Bay Estuary is a bird-watcher's heaven. People can watch the blue heron, osprey, and snowy egret along the miles of shoreline. It is also well-known for the high concentration of winter eagles.

5

What do the North Pole and Jefferson, New Hampshire, have in common?

Answer: They are both home to Santa Claus. The attraction in Jefferson has pulse-pounding rides, magic shows, an elf university to learn the tricks of their trade, shows in which toys come to life, and visits with Santa. Jefferson's attraction is open varying hours from May to October and then reopens from November through Christmas.

6

Where is the longest covered bridge in the United States?

Answer: The longest covered bridge is in New Hampshire. The Cornish-Windsor Bridge is 450 feet long.

7

What did a Concord man invent in 1787?

Answer: Levi Hutchins invented the first alarm clock in 1787.

8

What did New Hampshirite Earl Tupper invent?

Answer: Earl Tupper, born in Berlin, New Hampshire, became well known for inventing small plastic containers called "Tupperware."

FOR MORE INFORMATION

Books

Casbin, Linda, ed. *Fodor's 2002 Maine, Vermont, New Hampshire*. New York: Fodor's Travel Publications Inc., 2001.

Muse, Vance. *The Smithsonian Guide to Historic America: Northern New England*. New York: Stewart, Tabori & Chang Inc., 1989.

Otfinoski, Steven. *New Hampshire*. Celebrate the States Series. New York: Benchmark Books, 1999.

Web Sites

You can also go online and have a look at the following Web sites:

General Information
http://www.50states.com/newhampshire.htm

New Hampshire Tourism
http://www.visitnh.gov

State Information
http://www.officialcitysites.org/newhampshire.htm

Some Web sites stay current longer than others. To find other New Hampshire Web sites, enter search terms such as "New Hampshire," "Concord," "The Granite State," or any other topic you want to research.

GLOSSARY

ancestry: family line; the people from whom an individual or group is descended

beryl: a precious stone that is usually green

caboose: the last car on a freight train

constitution: the laws and principles under which a government runs a state or country

Continental Army: the name of the United States Army during the American Revolution

diverse: made up of different kinds

endangered: at risk of becoming extinct

glaciers: large rivers of ice that move very slowly

honorary: given high regard

hydroelectric: using waterpower to create electricity

presidential primary election: an election to choose a political party's presidential candidate

quarry: an open pit from which stone is mined

railroad ties: wooden beams laid between railroad tracks to support the rails

revolutionary: a person or group committed to political or social change

wigwams: huts or tents made by attaching skins or mats over a framework of poles

INDEX